Accents Of
INTIMACY

A COLLECTION OF POEMS AND DEVOTIONALS

WRITTEN BY

SHALONDA TRENT

To order additional copies of this book, contact:
Xlibris
844-714-8691
www.Xlibris.com
Orders@Xlibris.com

NIV
Scripture quotations marked NIV are taken from the Holy Bible, New International Version®. NIV®. Copyright © 1973, 1978, 1984 by International Bible Society. Used by permission of Zondervan. All rights reserved. [Biblica]

KJV
Scripture quotations marked KJV are from the Holy Bible, King James Version (Authorized Version). First published in 1611. Quoted from the KJV Classic Reference Bible, Copyright © 1983 by The Zondervan Corporation.

ISBN: Softcover   978-1-6641-8848-8
        EBook   978-1-6641-8849-5

Print information available on the last page

Rev. date: 08/04/2021

ACCENTS OF
INTIMACY

FOREWORD

Accents of intimacy is an example of what our heart's posture should mirror before the father. Transparent, real and desperate before the father, more sanctification, more passion, more accents of Intimacy.

Anonymous

CONTENTS

Free

No longer bound, by chains and fetters,
No longer moved hoping things will get better,
Cause better they have gotten and better they will be,

I am so happy to announce that I am free,
Free from empty hope, ropes, and chains,

Free from being a prisoner, lost, lonely and ashamed,

The old man is dead, the beast has been tamed,

A new picture in my life to be framed,
Living my life being all that I can be,

Note to self, I am free.

Devotional: What does it mean to be free?

I am reminded of my life before being converted, I had no boundaries within my life. To me, anything went, anything I felt like doing, I did it. Imagine this, I actually felt like I was free to do what I wanted to do, but in actuality, I was bound to my fleshly desires and demonic strongholds. The deceptive outlook on freedom viewed with the natural eye is carnal, but looking at it with the spiritual eye, being free is not being bound by anything that separates us from our purpose and divine relationship with Father Yahweh. I am reminded of the scripture in John 8:36 where it says,

"If the Son therefore shall make you free, ye shall be free indeed". (KJV)

Freedom is a beautiful thing, and once we obtain it through Messiah Yeshua we must cherish the freedom we have in him and share it with the world.

Prayer starter: Abba Father, I ask this day that you will purify my heart, mind, body, spirit and soul from anything that hinders me from being free or would hinder the freedom that I already have, strengthen my heart to hold fast the freedom that I now have in your precious and mighty name.

Sobeit.

The Prodigal

A shadow of the story of the prodigal son, running to the grace I use to run from,

Living a life of sin seemed fun for a season,

Found myself hopeless after while with nothing to believe in,

Suffocating from the stench of sin became difficult to breathe in,

Wallowing in the muck and mire, and then to be cast into hell fire?

Oh no, this couldn't be my lot, the life I was living I had to stop, so my pride had to drop, even though the enemy thought he had me on lock, I realized I was on redemption's clock,

Everyday that passed it was ticking, and the hour glass's sand trickling,

One day laying on the floor of an abandoned house, I thought to myself, my father's hired servants live better than this, I arose at once nothing else left to risk.

Because I was tired of letting the enemy's fists meet blows to my face, I chose to chase the master, and forget about everything that would proceed after.

Running and chasing after him faster and faster, and he met me in the way with open arms, he gave me a new robe and shoes to put on.

No longer a prodigal but adopted by grace, now I can run this divine destined race.

Devotional: The poem above is a mirror and picture of what my life use to be, before receiving deliverance. I remember sitting on the floor in an abandoned house I was sleeping in and thinking to myself, I must arise and go to my father's house, because I don't have to live like this. Before I go any further, I want to highlight the particular scripture that correlates with the poem, "Prodigal".

Luke 15:17 (NIV), "When he came to his senses, he said, 'How many of my father's hired servants have food to spare, and here I am starving to death! [18] I will set out and go back to my father and say to him: Father, I have sinned against heaven and against you. [19] I am no longer worthy to be called your son; make me like one of your hired servants.' [20] So he got up and went to his father.

HaleluYah how amazing is that? For those of you who aren't familiar with Luke 15:11-32, the story Is about a son who asked of his father for his inheritance, so his father gave it to him. After the son received his inheritance he went out and got entangled with riotous living and spent his money on women and things that had no profit. After all his money was gone and the sin he participated in, no longer was fun (sin is only pleasurable for a season), he came to himself. My Yah, he came to himself, I just want to focus on that part, "he came to himself, to his senses. It's amazing that when we are in our mess people can talk to us and encourage us, even pray for us, but until we let go and heed the father's voice and come to ourselves, we are still yet in our sins. But when an individual comes to their self, they have taken the power back they gave to the enemy, and then have the power after repenting to return to the side of the father.

How amazing is that? To have been separated from our heavenly father to being reconciled is truly beautiful. The father loves us on today and for those of you who haven't returned to the father as of yet and you want to welcome him into your heart let us pray this prayer,

Prayer starter: Heavenly father, I have strayed, I have been separate from the joy of your salvation, I pray that you guide me back to you, so that I can enjoy sweet fellowship with you and in the name of Yeshua I command the enemy to release me in Yeshua's name.

Sobeit.

Oh, My Creator, Heal My Heart!

It's evident there has been a shift from the start,

Oh wretched being I am,

It's my heart,
Deceitful and wicked always wanting,

Never satisfied, taking me for a ride to a place,

To expensive to stay,

So I sway, and say that I'll never have to pay,

But I do, so many a dozen have fallen,

My heart is hungry and for you, it is calling,

Oh my creator, we are in need of your love and direction,

We steal, kill, cheat, and beat,

We envy our brother's and sister's table in which they eat,
We await opportunity and to take someone's seat.

But I'll lay at your feet, everything that I need,

I need purity of spirit,

Purity of heart, it's evident to me there's been a shift from the start,

Oh, my creator!, heal. . . . . . . .heal our hearts.

Devotional: Anyone that has ever lived or breathed on this side of life has experienced some form of pain within the heart. Rather someone inflicted it upon us, or we have inflicted it upon ourselves, it hurts. Can you believe that when we are outside of the will of the father he will allow our hearts to go through and suffer pain, so that we can call out to him and ask for his help to get back into alignment with him. There are all kinds of pains in this life, even living a righteous life the bible says it is impossible that offences will come, but woe to him through whom they come (Luke 17:1). So we can always rest assure that the father will be with us, lead us, and guide us into greener pastures (Psalm 23:2).

Prayer starter: Heavenly Father, Oh, my creator, guide and direct the feet of us, your children, help us to discern your leading, purify our hearts and hands to your service in the precious name of your Son, Yeshua, sobeit.

Oh, Wounded Heart

Oh wounded heart tossed with tempest and wind,

Be encouraged my friend, for love you will know again,

Be not worried, dismayed or scared,

For the scars you've been acquainted with and the endless tears,
Do you not know from water, do flowers grow?
Blossom and emit?
For you will see health and healing you can't resist,
Stay focused and encouraged, let not the door of where you stay stoop low,
For you were wounded and have traveled were many often go.
But back you shall return, from the bruises and the burns.
For you my heart often yearns to learn, lessons the pain couldn't afford to earn,

Cry not neither let sorrow befriend you, for a wounded heart, a healed heart shall mend you.

Psalm 51:10 (K.IV)

"Create in me a clean heart,O Yahweh;and renew a right spirit within me."

Prayer Starter: Abba Yahweh, mend every broken heart, you know the pain that each and every individual has gone through and faced. You alone can heal and restore and relieve every ache, I claim healing for every individual that is reading this, you will love again, you will begin again, you will also trust again in the mighty name of Yeshua.

Sobeit.

Release

Oh how the heart does cry and scream,
Often for the things that mean me no good,
Oh how bitter the taste of pain in my mouth,
As I felt us drift apart,

Today the loins of my stomach are girded,
I am learning how to let go and see him,
As healing grows, the pain the tears brought has built a priceless gift no money could have ever bought.

For my heart I sought, for myself I searched, digging through layers of hurt, I found a skirt dingy with sin,

I ran to the altar repented and let him in,
From here I shall excel, and move on with joy,

I disregard the chatter, off to a new chapter.
Looking forward to the latter.

Psalm 55:22 (KJV)

Cast thy burden upon Yahweh, and he shall sustain thee.

Prayer starter: Abba Father, we release every thought and care before you today, we cast our burdens upon you, for you will sustain us, we know you to be a heavy load bearer and we come to lay it all down at your feet and receive your peace in exchange for our load. Sobeit

Happiness

Having

Absolutely

Pampering

Periods

In

Newness

Everyday

Smiling

Going All The Way

I'm going all the way,
I'm not turning back,
No more shall my feet halt,
Not looking back as to turn into salt,
If I seem zealous, it's not my fault,
Blame the one who changed me,

Purged and rearranged me, namely Yeshua the Messiah,
He came into my heart,
Showed me how to love, showed me how to care,
Showed me I could live a life without fear,
He showed me how to excel and expel every
Spell the enemy tried to cast,
Everyone of his plans to hell went back,
I'm not going back,

Letting my passion take over, I willn not need to fight in this battle, but I'll hold my peace to say the least,

On his body and blood will I feast,
My heart I release, screaming no more sheets!
I shall lay at his feet, no more defeat, living like the meek, his face will I seek,

I'm going all the way, tomorrow and today,
Yesterday and forever, no more wet tears of sorrow on my sweater,
He whispered a word that it's only getting better,
Because I chose going all the way.

Philippians 3:13-14 (KJV)

[13] Brethren, I count not myself to have apprehended: but this one thing I do, forgetting those things which are behind, and reaching forth unto those things which are before,

[14] I press toward the mark for the prize of the high calling of Yahweh in Messiah Yeshua.

Devotional: Being a believer doesn't mean we will not make mistakes, but it does mean we have power to overcome anything that life throws our way, we even have power to surrender all of our members to the Father, through His Son Yeshua. I love how the Apostle Paul put it that he doesn't count his self to have arrived. He doesn't count himself as one that is not subject to error, but he said this one thing I do, forgetting those things which are behind. Forgetting those ways, people, places and things. Yes, those unhealthy and sinful habits that proved detrimental to our soul salvation. We do not have to do it alone, we have a Comforter (John 14:16). Divine guidance and direction available to us, but we have to want it and submit to that guidance.

Prayer Starter: Abba Father, I desire to go all the way, I desire to submit every one of my members to you that you may live through me, for I am dead and my life is hid in your Son, direct my heart to rejoice in you and not to,lose heart when difficult times arise but rather keep my mind set on going all the way.

Stripes

Conviction is the friction, that kept me up all night,
The reason why the battle wasn't short of a fight,
Writing wrongs wrong, making rights right,

It all ties back to the stripes on his back,
I didn't have to ask if such salvation would last,
Cause he said that it wouldn't be abolished forever,
His word, love letter, no more bitter tasting tears drenching my sweater, his love is the trendsetter,
He freed the prisoners who were captive in fetters,

No headers or intros he took blows,
He didn't fold, but as a lamb dumb before her shearers, he opened not his mouth,

The stripes on his back we knew nothing about,
They say it's ok, we say it's fine, but time can't define reading between the lines,
Bought with a price, brought to the light, every day is a fight,

Reaching different heights, scared? Not the slight,
It all ties to the stripes he wore on his back,
Not knowing how to react,

To transact and put it into order with facts,
To be heard like you never have before, score, his blood, his love, from above no wishing on
stars, wish if you may wish if you might, it ALL is included in his stripes.

Galatians 6:17 (KJV)

From henceforth let no man trouble me: for I bear in my body the marks of Yeshua The
Messiah.

Devotional: Isn't that amazing? To be given such a sacrifice as heaven's best? Even Yeshua (Jesus) The Messiah . The stripes he wore on his back for us, has given us the privilege to look back at what he suffered to set us free from being bound to the sinful nature. Because of his stripes we are healed, and we are justified by faith (not justified to continue in sin Romans 6), but justified to be declared the righteousness of Yahweh, being set free from our past and the mistakes that we have made. Being given new life, a new slate, and a new start.

Prayer starter: Abba Father, I come to you to thank you for your Son's stripes that he wore on Calvary for me. He paid the price for my sins and took the death that I, myself deserved that I might have right to the tree of life. I am bursting with joy and happiness, I pray that you ignite the fire of zeal for you within me. Sobeit.

Remember

I'll remember how you kept me,

Remember how you swept me, right off my feet,

I was found singing a new song,

With a new beat,

No more defeat, or feet that cannot move,

No more living by the law with rules,

I'm out, I'm open, I'm ready, and I'm focused,

As I go, I'll remember the pressure, remember the fight,

I'll remember the thoughts that kept me up at night,

I'll remember the revelation, in my heart that shines bright,

I'll remember the moment, remember the mic,

Naysayers and haters, upset with the favor,

Shown to me through grace, just trying to run my race,

Anticipating the day that I'll see his face,

Running at a different pace, taking victory treads that can be traced,

I'll remember your faithfulness and splendor, I'll remember, remember, remember.

Isaiah 43:26 (KJV)

Put me in remembrance: let us plead together; declare thou, that thou mayest be justified.

Devotional: It is absolutely relieving that the father has invited us to put him in remembrance. He declared in verse 25 of Isaiah 43, that he is Yahweh who has blot out our transgressions, even he. He has given us an opportunity to put these life changing revelations into remembrance so that we will be built up on our most holy faith.

Prayer starter: Abba Father today, I intentionally put you in remembrance, that I may be justified. I put you in remembrance because I have found it so easy to forget in my flesh. Direct my memory to never forget, but hold fast to the remembrance of your Holy name. Sobeit.

Devotional: Who Are We Intimate With?

When you think of intimacy what comes to mind?

When I think of intimacy, I think of something along the lines of a close knit togetherness. Something speaking in natural terms that a married couple with engage in. And it not necessarily means just sex, but just spending time with one another, listening to how each other's day has gone, a romantic date or working out with one another. When it comes to who we are intimate with, it indicates and reveals where we are in our spiritual walk with Father Yahweh (God). To go a step further, if we are intimate with demonic spirits we are committing spiritual adultery. I am reminded of Ahola and Aholibah.

Ezekiel 23:1-4 (KJV)

1The word of Yahweh came again unto me, saying, 2Son of man, there were two women, the daughters of one mother: 3 And they committed whoredoms in Egypt; they committed whoredoms in their youth: there were their breasts pressed, and there they bruised the teats of their virginity. 4 And the names of them were Aholah the elder, and Aholibah her sister: and they were mine, and they bare sons and daughters. Thus were **their names; Samaria** is Aholah, and Jerusalem Aholibah.

And so, these two women symbolized how Samaria and Jerusalem committed whoredoms.

Even so, spiritually we can be subject to spiritually stepping out of our marriage covenant with our heavenly father. So you may ask, how can I steer clear of doing this?

I can only speak from a place of experience and I have been saved and delivered for over ten years. I have been in a place of committing spiritual adultery, and let me tell you it wasn't a good place to be. What really helped, is the love of the father. He was ever so patient with me. I had a mind to do what I wanted to do and backslid. In that place the only one who could get through to me, was the father. In spite of how much my heart had hardened I knew within myself, that every chastening I was facing, is because he loved me. The things I went through because of disobedience, was the fruit of my doings, and I got tired of living a life contrary to the will of the father.

My goodness, when we stop running and being so set in our ways, that gives the father a chance to work on us and revive us back to life.

Prayer starter: Abba Father Yahweh (God) guide me to your side, I want to engage in fellowship with you, that allows me to experience you in an intimate way that conforms me to your image. Help me to trust the process. Guide me to trust in you and not lean upon my own understanding. Sobeit.

No More Pressure

I have heard that pressure bust pipes,

The reason why my spirit didn't have peace within the night,

Every day's a struggle, every day's a fight,

Battling in the spirit, darkness against the light,

Past against the present, and now I can see it,

Many times we have a dream, but not bold to receive it,

In the dream, I believe it, I have a baby growing in the inside called destiny,

It's time to conceive it, that isw called conception,

I leave my past behind, that is called neglection,

No more pressure no more pain,
Singing sorrowful blues in the rain,

No more doing things in vain,
But whatever I do unto him in his name,

He set me free, he loosed the chains,

Bondage rope broken, he did it all,
No more pressure or intoxicated anxiety,
I claim sobriety,

Even though the devil's eyeing me,
It doesn't matter I have EL- Shaddai
With me.

Prayer starter: Abba father, I am so glad that your are omnipotent and omniscient. I never want to take for granted that I can lay everything at your feet. I pray that the Holy Spirit will continue to guide me to lay everything at your feet, not some but everything, so that I can enjoy the gift of salvation without feeling weighed down. Sobeit.

What He Is Doing For Me

He brought me close and hugged me so tight,

That everything that was attached to me that was dead, shrieked at the sight of eternal life himself, fell at my feet and shriveled up. His embrace gave me so much life and hope. He helped me to understand that pain is not always a negative thing. Pain is not always something that causes you to be weak, but it can if you let it; deposit a strength in you, you never knew existed.

2 Corinthians 12:9 (KJV)

And he said unto me, My grace is sufficient for thee: for my strength is made perfect in weakness. Most gladly therefore will I rather glory in my infirmities, that the power of Messiah may rest upon me.

Prayer starter : Heavenly Father, I am so glad that your strength is made perfect in weakness, I am so glad that you reign and are seated, and your Son is seated on the right hand of you in victory. I bless your holy name today and commit my works unto you that my thoughts may be established. Sobeit.

Taking It Back

I'm taking back my peace, I'm taking back my life,

I'm taking back everything you stole from me,

Like a thief in the night,

No longer will I be a captive to my feelings,

Enslaved by my emotions, in bondage deep within,

I'm taking back my happiness, yes I'm taking back my joy,

I come to take everything, because I've grown annoyed,

I'm not afraid of walking side by side with the one responsible for the peace I have inside,

I'm taking back tonight,
Everything that seems right,

As long as I'm still free, cause honestly, that's all that matters to me.

John 8:36 (KJV)

If the Son therefore shall make you free, ye shall be free indeed.

Prayer starter: Heavenly Father, I thank you today that I can take back what I gave away to satan. I thank you Abba for your redemptive power through your Son Yeshua the Messiah that leads me into abundant life worth living in you. Help me as I take everything back, to never give it away again. Sobeit

Put Yahweh First

Not second to last but first,
Even when it hurts and you want to let your flesh work and flirt,

Put Yahweh First, when the hug closes in and you know we're more than friends,

Put Yahweh first, when passion arises and intensifies, Let Yah arise.

Waiting is not something usually greeted with a smile,

But I trust the master's way,
And know it'll be worthwhile,

So next time we cross paths, let's remember this for sure and take heed,

That if we say we love him, we will listen to him indeed,

His word, meditate and read, and delight in the bread of life,

Because once you get a taste everything will be alright,

Not in feeling, or sight in the flesh,
But our faith and dedication, the master must put
To the test,
I confess it's not easy, but worth it, it is,
No more childish games as kids, foolishness let's rid,

Our hearts in him must be hid, even when it's late, your in the mood and it hurts, remember these words,

Put Yahweh first.

2 Timothy 2:22 (KJV)

Flee also youthful lusts: but follow righteousness, faith, charity, peace, with them that call on Yahweh out of a pure heart.

Prayer starter: Heavenly Father, its not easy denying the flesh daily, it's not easy abstaining from fleshly lusts which war against the soul, though the flesh is weak, your Spirit indeed is willing. Help me to surrender to you even when it's difficult.

Breaking Out

No longer will I be a captive to my past,
If they should ever ask,

Sometime short- term expectations do not last,

Breaking out didn't break, so its not out of style,

Here's a moment, here's a thought to ponder on for a while,

While the rain of life doesn't stop pouring because of umbrellas and rain boots,

So the unprepared are drenched in the soak of regret,

Because one didn't prepare for the rain, though it came,

Sunshine came too, those who ready stepped out, I don't blame you,

I name you wise, you claimed the prize,
The early bird gets the worm,
Breaking out past limits, the limits I had in my past,

Made up my mind to run pass the finish line,
Now is my time!

No more will I be an inmate in the prison of limits and settling,

On the ground like Jacob with the angel wrestling,

Not letting go until I get my blessing, persistence taught me a lesson,

Slothfulness no longer a profession, in the boxing ring of life,

A new contestant, no longer chained down by the spirit of depression,

I know it's a lot like a confession, I'm breaking out pass self,

To gain a wealth that money cannot buy, and saving can't save it, but if I'm saved I can receive it,

Can you believe it? If so, then retrieve it,
My heart is shouting out, here I go, here I am, Hello,
Breaking out.

Isaiah 52:9 (KJV) Break forth into joy, sing together, ye waste places of Jerusalem: for Yahweh hath comforted his people, he hath redeemed Jerusalem.

Prayer starter: Abba Father, I am so grateful that through your power I can break forth. I can press past limitations and a low way of thinking and my desire is that you never allow me to be comfortable in anything less than what you have for me.

True Discipleship

Go to church?
So does Satan,

Preach the word?
So does Satan,

Know the bible?
So does Satan,

Do good deeds?
So Does Satan,

Member of the choir?
So is Satan,

Believe in Yahweh?
So does Satan,

You may ask well, what would make me a true disciple of Yeshua (Jesus)?

Ok, I'll tell you, there's one thing satan can't do, and that's walk in love.

1 John 4:20 (KJV)If a man say, I love Yahweh, and hateth his brother, he is a liar: for he that loveth not his brother whom he hath seen, how can he love Yahweh whom he hath not seen?

Devotional: Gracious king, you know and discern the hearts of the children of men, you understand our frame, purify our hearts, that all we do, our labor is not in vain. Help us that our heart's posture is right with you and that all we do is to your glory and not for anything else. Sobeit.

I Rather It Be Him

I could write about the moon, outer space and the stars,

I could write about how near, close by, or how far,

I could write about a man, a kiss, or a date,

I could write about love, jealousy and hate,

But I would rather, write about my king,
How he hung, bled and died,

For all of our sins, and has risen again,

I could write about depression, or how I think I am smart,

But I rather write about the ones who made it over adorned in white,

Who will sing and shout, about the win and the fight,

Of how they pressed and trusted, through persecutions and tests,

What a day, what a day, it will be in the sky,
The day in which we will no longer wonder or question why,

I rather give him glory, as I tell my story,

It may seem corny, but unashamed I'll tell it all,

I'll tell it on the mountain tops, roofs and in the markets,

Come see a man who told me all I ever did!

I rather step aside, let him work and be patient,

Was created for such a time and selfless statement.

Prayer starter: Abba no matter what I obtain in this life, help me to be ever aware that I give you all the glory and honor due to your name, because if it hadn't been for you, I would have never accomplished anything. I recognize that and I Honor your holy name. Sobeit.

It's All For Him

No glory or recognition to me, but to the one who gave me eyes to see,

See cause I believe he often doesn't get what he deserves in spite of what we've heard,

But he can and he will,
Yet and still I don't feel it, but I know,
He deserves the glory, so I will let it show,

Every good and perfect gift comes from the father from above,

Who gave it freely and in love,

So my gifts I yield to him, who I count a faithful friend,

Who will well out live everything to the end,

The victory I have, every door, every win,
The door of my heart I left open, he came in,

I don't need the likes, because I have his love,
Fellowship with him, to me, is enough,

Every poem, every quote, love letter and note,

I dedicate it to Yahweh, Elohim, My King,

To him belongs all these things,

Glory, Honor, Strength, Dominion and power.

Devotional: In this life, we often are faced with a thing called pride. We often forget our humble beginnings, when we get what we pray for. I remember when I was a babe in the Messiah. I knew in my heart that he had greater things for me, and so I would fear walking into it, because I didn't want to become prideful or haughty. But after while, I realized that I couldn't allow the spirit of fear to hinder me from walking into everything the father has for me. I have faith today, that whatever he has allowed me to have, he has given me the grace, to handle it. You too can believe and have faith that the father will direct your heart in all of your endeavors. Even when the spirit of pride tries to rise up we have power to rebuke that spirit. I take this personal because I know where the father has delivered and brought me from. From homosexuality, alcohol and other drugs, depression, bitterness, homelessness and so much more. So when people see the new me, and they see the glow, when they see the books or the things that I may have, I always aim to walk in a spirit of humility, because I know it's because of his grace. Before I gave my life to the father, I had nothing, not so much as even a high school diploma (which I later obtained). But since giving my life to him apart from a college education, and many more opportunities, he's given me new life. He's given me a clean slate, forgiving me of all my sins, and casting it into the sea of forgetfulness! HaleluYAH so when I think of his goodness and faithfulness towards me my heart becomes overwhelmed in gratefulness in boasting in him, never myself. See because when you have been so bound and lost and you get set free, it's quite sobering. You know that the thing that has happened to you, yourself is not responsible for.

So because of that, it makes you appreciate your freedom, even more. Aren't you glad about being free? In spite of what the enemy throws our way to hurt us, it ends up making us better and we continue to grow in grace and come up higher.

There is nothing more precious than being given new life, and then turning around and sharing that with the world. I want to encourage someone right now, the lies the enemy has whispered in your ear is a lie. When he told you that you were nothing and wasn't going to finish your degree, he was lying! He is the father of lies, if you weren't powerful and important to the father, the devil wouldn't be fighting so hard to keep you out of a mindset of victory.

Prayer starter: Abba Father, you are mighty in battle, I love the way you operate and move, like nobody can. So because of that, all the glory and honor belongs to you and only you. Help me to always give it to you, and shun the very appearance of evil and the spirit of pride.

Sobeit.

Fragments Of A Scattered Heart

Glimpses of communion with the Savior draw me nearer,

I was blinded by the cares of this world,

But now I see it clearer, even when I thought doubtless I had made it,

Time could only tell, as the passion faded,

My heart by the world's system was misguided and aided by anecdotes overrated,

I do now hate it, the texts bings and things grabbing my attention away,

From the only hope I know, so I am left with the realization,

That my king has been patient, and now I gather the fragments of a scattered heart,

Pieces over here, pieces over there, anchored in emptiness and desolation,

I have made up my mind, to take my time, and take advantage of full restoration,

When your heart is scattered, so are your thoughts and dreams,

But to Yahweh's understanding will I lean,

If this world's way was enough it wouldn't leave me hungry for more,

I have searched high and low for the fragments of my scattered heart,
with beliefs that it will be aided back to wholeness again,

No more tossed to and fro, without knowing where to go,

I tried once finding the fragments to piece it all together,

But I found the only thing that could make it better, was in the letter of grace, liberty and faith,

No more chasing waste, I dispose of the taste,
Yahweh I have made up my mind to seek your face,

Which results to peace and rest, no more attaching burdens to my chest,

The fragments are here, and oh, are they dear,
I yield them to you, no hesitation or fear.

Often in life our hearts can become scattered by things that have been done to us, or things we inflict on ourselves. But no matter what causes our pain or the fragments of our hearts that may scatter, aren't you grateful that the father, has the power to put it back together? And of course, we play apart as well, we still have to do our work, that he won't do. It's very important to understand that. I remember a season in my life where I thought I was waiting for the father to do something regarding an employment opportunity, but through trial and error, I learned that faith without works is dead. So as the father is willing to mend and restore, we have to do our part too, and he will even help us with that.

Prayer starter: Gracious matchless King, you are the mender of broken hearts, and you are a healer, help me to do my work and be consistent in doing it for my good, and your glory.

Sobeit.

Reach

I will reach for not the stars, but will reach pass far, and beyond infinity time is an entity who befriended me,

I did not understand how to appreciate such a relationship, so wasted time did I, But as was it was wasted,

No time to cry, or let opportunity again walk by, I will reach for what I may not comprehend,

Cause in the end, at least I was taught not to have empty-handed dreams,

And so it seems that this means I'll have to lift my arms and disarm the intoxicating lie that I'd be harmed,

But all along, that was a lie, not through airplane, rocket, or any other man-made device,

But I choose to reach by faith, for to me that's the only way that seems right.

Prayer starter: Yahweh of heaven and earth I know that the sky is not the limit, for you made the sky and everything that has been made. You are well able to guide your children to never reach for things that are easily obtained, but for the things that may require more of us and our submission to you. Lead us your children to reach higher for you, to reach higher to receive the things you have prepared for them that love you, Sobeit.

You Can't Have My Voice

I'm taking it back, I have no other choice, you can't have my voice,

Passivity passed on, I buried her and gave her a benediction,

I am not afraid of the friction of telling you no,
I choose to reap a harvest, I have diligently sown,

My voice is mines so leave me alone, everyday your behind me breathing trying to plant fear,

But I served fear an eviction notice, it doesn't live here,

I will speak the word of Yahweh, much more will I live,

I am a woman who lost her voice and got it back,
I'm in the race which is faith, and you can't stop my tracks,

I have power according to the first chapter of acts,

When you try to provoke me, with faith I'll react,

Yahweh made a deposit, now it's time to transact,

So for this I will rejoice, and I'll say it again,
You know who you are, you can't have my voice.

Prayer Starter: Abba I thank you for giving me the strength to take my voice back. I thank you that the mouths of your people will not be muzzled, but we will cry aloud and spare not, and shew your people their transgressions. Sobeit.

Who Am I?

Who am I, that I should have power and stature or room in a prominent place?,

Who am I that I should have on silk slippers
And a robe inscribed with an s on the left in purple?,

Am I not only a servant to serve Yahweh and his people?
Who am I that I should have gold plated necklaces and jewelry in galore,

Or ivory pillars in my house and jaded marble floors?

Should I not count myself with those who have not?
To become less to be more,
Or what is it worth, if not given to the rest,
Who may be less fortunate than I,
Because who am I to see my brother or sister in need and walk right by?

This is my reply, I will put my lot in with the lowly,

For I am not too high,
After all, who am I?

Proverbs 18:12 (KJV)

Before destruction the heart of man is haughty, and before honour is humility.

Prayer starter: Abba, I pray that you revive the spirit of man in your humility. Help us to stay in a mindset of lowliness through your Ruach Hakodesh, for without your Spirit can we do nothing.

Sobeit.

Heart Of Gold

Oh my heart, as it sat in disarray,

Not knowing which words to say,

I cried out to abba, oh abba I pray,

My heart is here for you to mold,

Take this heart and make it a heart of gold,

I ask not amissly, anything that doesn't honor you

Can miss me,

I invite your love to kiss me, and bliss me, please don't resist me,

My heart is broken, and my spirit contrite, fix me upright,

Oh this heart has known many scars, but you oh Abba have brought me this far,

This is not to cry in sorrow without a cause, I will wait yet listen and pause, as the blessings and favor unfold, I give you my heart,

To mold, into a heart of gold,

The Savior's Face

As I peered at the wall, my heart suddenly stalled,
I looked away amazed,
The holy Spirit instructed me to stare,
I did with an earnest heart and much care.
As I studied his face, it wore such pain,
He gave his all in order to gain,
Saving me and you was his aim.

On his face was deep agony and sorrow,
But he hung there on the tree in hopes of tomorrow, and the third day to be exact
Many whips and lashes wore his back,
Just to reconcile us back, on his head was a crown of thorns,
As blood trickled down his face and every other place,
This is the night I saw the Savior's face,
Where his mouth was a rainbow shining bright,
I will never ever forget that night,
The rainbow signifies promise, the promise that he made,
That he will be with us always and return again some day,
On the wall, I saw tears and the power as they dropped,
That day on Calvary he accomplished a lot
So my question to you, is have you reserved your spot?
To be seated in heavenly places and to be given a new heart?
Confessing our sins is the beginning of the start,
Let us not live off of maybes or something along the lines of might,
I know in my heart I could never forget the night,
That I saw the Savior's face.

Ishi

You have betrothed me unto you, I have received your love letter dipped in your blood as I taste your silhouette kisses,

No more reminiscing on Egypt. Where I claimed I ate good, paying that old mean Pharoah homage, as if he cared.
For I was ensnared and laden with hard bondage and labor.
As the daughter of Zion I cried out, to my Ishi. Yes it is true, I went whoring after other gods, that
cannot breathe or arise to my rescue. I needed a Savior so I stepped out the way and let you,
Do what no other can do, you stepped in and made my heart new,
Ishi, for I have heard your voice in an acceptable time, my heart's rhythm now beats to
your movement. Since you have taken me as yours I see clear improvement,
Ishi, from the mountain tops will I proclaim I am no longer on the market, we have
exchanged vows and have entered into holy matrimony a covenant so special,

My love Ishi, yes my husband you are, you have sought me long and very far,
No more are you to me Baali, but I shall forever call you Ishi, for I am betrothed to you.

Hosea 2:16 (KJV)

And it shall be at that day, saith YHWH, that thou shalt call me Ishi;and shalt call me no more Baali.

How amazing is that? To be betrothed and married to the king of glory. It can be often viewed as a cliché, however if we really open our hearts, and embrace this powerful revelation, of the father being married to the believer, we will experience an intimacy we have never even knew existed.

Prayer Starter: Father Yahweh today, I come before you to acknowledge you as Ishi, my husband. So, because you are my husband guide my heart to honor and please you, making mention of your name in everything that I truly open my heart to intimacy with you, and that I allow you to love on me the way I really need it today. Sobeit.

Devotional: To be betrothed to Father Yahweh is a beautiful thing, he has married us and we have entered into a marriage covenant with him. It's so refreshing to know we are his, and he is ours. Like any marriage, our husbands are our covering, they help and aide us in things that we may not understand or discern. Husbands are the head of the relationship, and speaking from a natural perspective, it's so important that a man be led by the Spirit of Yahweh, because if he isn't he will lead his wife into the ditch.

Prayer starter: Abba Father, I know more call you Baali, but I now call you Ishi, my husband. You have proven to be faithful to this marriage covenant, and have shown me that you are my true covering. Abba, I pray that you help me to be a faithful wife to you and my future husband, purify my heart as I engage in accents of intimacy with you. Sobeit.

You Are Welcome

Perfect gentleman, not rushing to override,

But I know from the way you pursue me that you want to come inside,

You want to come inside and make your abode,

To take up residence within me, I love the way you move not caring if you offend me,

Or my emotions, that is why I come to you being honest and open.

I am tired of holding back from you what's rightfully yours.

For you are the way, the truth, even the door.

So I open to you yearning for more. I am not satisfied with just a taste.

I cannot wait until the day I shall meet you face to face.

My heart is panting my throat is quite dry. But I will continue my search no matter how low no matter how far.

I will reach pass the stars Jupiter and Mars, my heart is on a mission to take the transition,

I'm done with intermissions and switching from having one foot in.

Sold out is what you want, sold out is what you get,

I can't let my heart wander any longer my Elohim, You are welcome.

Devotional: My goodness, when we welcome the father into our hearts, it's a beautiful thing. But look at where you were before conversion. We didn't like when the father would step in and ruin our plans to continue in a life of sin. But, when our eyes and heart were enlightened, we ran to the grace, we use to run from! HaleluYAH! That's what you call saving grace, that leads and enables us to say father, you are welcome. Father you are welcome to guide me, you are welcome into the rooms of my heart I used to leave off-limits to you, because when our hearts are constrained by the Holy Spirit, we only want him to have access to everything concerning us.

Prayer starter: Gracious King, I invite you today into my heart yet again. I say thank you to you for even chasing me who was disobedient and rebellious to your way and your word. I feel so honored to have you within my life. I am so grateful you have sought me as a shepherd does his sheep. Guide me to your side, and I won't fail to uplift and amplify your name. Sobeit.

I'm Not Ashamed

I'm not ashamed of the pain that stained my heart,

I'm not ashamed of the name by which I am called,

I am a daughter, and I'm not ashamed,

I'll proclaim and claim, standby and reply,

And if it doesn't apply let it fly, reason why? Is I'm not ashamed.

I won't reserve time to explain, but will not it extraordinarily plain. I'm not ashamed,

I'm not ashamed of the gospel, whose prophets and apostles have suffered for the truth,

And are sketched in heaven's roster, I'm not shamed, not afraid to proclaim or call on his holy name,

He keeps me sane; this is real life not a game,

I'm not ashamed,
I'm not ashamed,
I'm not ashamed.

Romans 1:16 (CSB) For I am not ashamed of the gospel, for it is the power of Yahweh for salvation to everyone who believes, to the Jew first and also to the Greek.

Devotional: The world we live in today is trying to convince and deceive us into thinking that wrong is right and right is wrong. It seems when bold believers speak up they are deemed to be " too deep" or "holier than thou". The truth is that's what the father wants us to be, on fire for him. He doesn't want for us to be afraid to speak out about what we know is the truth.

The bible instructs us to cry aloud and spare not. So why do some believers spare and some don't ? Why do some struggle to represent a holy life style and some have no problem with it ?

One of the reasons is feeling ashamed, not wanting to go through the persecutions that come with really following the Savior. Granted we are all not in the same place in our faith walk, that is why it is important to pray for one another and shame the devil. Shame those demons that whisper in our ears, "you don't have to do this, or you don't have to do that". Or " it doesn't take all that". Really? It doesn't take all of that? How can anyone speak to us about how much it takes to keep something we had to fight to receive? That they themselves probably haven't even received as of yet? That We had to fast to receive?

How can we allow that? The only one we can receive guidance from is the one who gave us this great salvation, and those he sends our way to guide and direct us. Because news flash salvation and receiving the Holy Spirit is a gift, that didn't come easy for most. But many want to live a sacrificial lifestyle. Oftentimes we want what we want. We want to pacify our flesh, instead of walking in the Spirit. That's the truth. That's why we cannot lean upon our own understanding, but upon his. The same thing it took to receive the blessing of salvation, is what it's going to take to keep and maintain it. The bible instructs us that strait is the gate and narrow is the way that leads to life, and few there be that find it. And again, it says wide is the gate and broad is the way that leads to destruction and many not few, but man y there be that go in that way (Matthew 7:13).

Prayer starter: Abba, guide my heart to follow you who is the way, the truth, and the life. I haven't been made perfect in the flesh, for you have saved and delivered me. Guide me to continue to know and follow your Son's lead in the precious name of Yeshua I pray, Sobeit.

I'm Springing

I'm springing from a place,

Of favor and grace,

Realistic goals as my purpose unfolds,

I leave behind my past, and things that didn't last,

Broke up with fear, faith is now here,

Gave a letter of divorcement to death and endorsements

That left a sister dormant,

No more hiding in corners afraid to break out,

I spring from a place you may know nothing about,

But I care to share not spare for embarrassment, from the pit I use to sit,

Upset at the preacher in the pulpit because my life wasn't fit,

I spring from a place, of mercy and of grace,

His face will I seek and chase,

Not looking for recognition,

This is a different edition, an addition to the friction

Of normalcy,

Being shaken up by greater and better, no more tears on my sweater,

I spring from a place of gratitude, busting down the door of destiny,

I know test and trials come to test me, get the best of me, so that it will flow,

Just a life tip, get faith and don't let it go,

When they irritate you, don't let it show,

This is real not for show,

I Spring, I blossom, I grow, I prosper, I emit.

Prayer starter: Gracious King from you do all blessings blossom and spring, help me today to allow your Spirit to lead and guide me until you spring from eternity, may your word spring from my heart that it may bless someone else in your precious and mighty name I pray, Sobeit.

Shalonda Trent born and raised in Waterbury,CT is a true example that Yeshua saves. Before her conversion she identified herself as a lesbian. She after years of running the streets and selling drugs, gave her life to Father Yahweh. She has had her ups and downs like any individual that has ever lived and prides on sharing her life experiences to encourage,uplift,admonish and edify. She is a stern believer of breaking pass the limits of statistics and limitations that we either place upon oursleves or what we allow others to place on us. "Have faith that it will happen" she says. Shalonda is a psychology major and believes that obtaining a higher education is very important. Growing up in an urban area and facing so many storms such as being hit by a car and almost dying, Shalonda is here for a reason and she has made up her mind to make everyday count.

Printed in the United States
by Baker & Taylor Publisher Services